When the Poppy Sheds

Poems of Recovery

Lindsay Gargotto

Least Bittern Books
Henry County, KY

Dedicated to my sister –
Kristen, Goddess of Waterfalls

Lindsay Gargotto wrote one poem on each of the first
30 days of her recovery. They are presented in the
order she wrote them.

Cover art and illustrations
by Bree in Pleasureville, KY
www.theartistBree.com

Least Bittern Books, an imprint
of Green Panda Press, publishes
trade paperbacks by poets with
strong, singular voices.

Inquiries to: greenpandapress@gmail.com

Least Bittern Books
147 Marcus St. #4
Pleasureville, KY
40057

the first 30 days

Day 1

Verification Day

I lay underneath a building,
bombed. Me. Just one morsel
left of the scorched-bitten gravel.
All of us here such tiny, tiny pieces.
Hundreds and hundreds of us can
fit in a single palm.
But my body never tried to move
from underneath the building.
I was a boulder, absolute.

I am an addict they want to hear me say,
I need to say.
I am a human being full of pain,
wrought in substances
that make me scorched less than a pebble,
too tiny for a palm to hold.

All the women here
are revisiting guests-
or is it recidivism?
Nine years sober, one week sober,
they all come back. The staff
are here when they come back.

I am fearful of everything.
With or without drugs I am alone
but at least here we are all made
of this building-
pebbles and boulders together.

Again (Day Two)

Dizzy. Asleep. Questions.
Sleep. Meals. Miss meals.
Finally shower.
No real soap. Art therapy.
A social worker. A doctor-
who says, " How does someone
like you, who does the work
you do, end up here?"
No answer again from Jason.
Insanity. Sleep again.

Day 3

Voices of the Night

It is another day.
My vision is becoming
milked-out clear.
Each of us mothers
with no home and empty
with no children
surrounding us,
but not
forgetting us-
a blessing
or a curse.

They say tell your child
bedtime stories in the womb.
They will never forget your voice.
But what happens when you
forget theirs?

I have lived two worlds,
as a mother and addict -
one of life and one of death.
My soul can no longer divide.

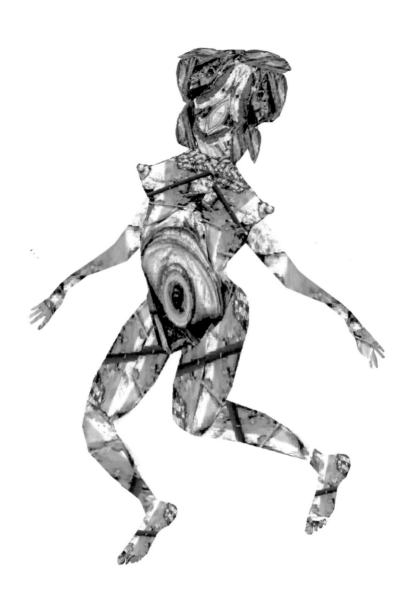

For Politicians (Day Four)

I am in the service
of myself, alone –
with a camp of warriors
and deserters.

The guards watch us,
count us, smile at us,
medicate us, command us.

The War on Drugs
is not on the streets.
Politicians are an allergy
like alcohol.

Day 5

Slipped

Begrudged faces revolving

room to room
screaming
through the doors

as if
we always run drill.

Finally
one face slipped still.
She stopped with a smile.
My face moved.

Me & Scarecrow (Day Six)

Disease: A particular quality, habit, or disposition regarded as adversely affecting a person or group of people.

Like the Scarecrow
the Wizard has filled me
with brains made of straw,
pins, needles, and such.
And I was ever so thankful.
Imaginary, delusionary, illusionary.

I am not quite sure
if my frontal lobe is cerebral anymore,
or my hypothalamus is synthesized
or my neurons are synapsed.
But does someone like me,
diseased, need these things
anyway?

Ergo, me & the Scarecrow
will forever share
the greatest fear together.

Bruised Breaths (Day Seven)

Come find your soul
    in this well of darkness
still filled with wishes
none of which should still be alive
    but with our bruised breaths
we still get to make wishes.

Day 8

Pity Me

I follow the light only
when I can feel it. I am
analytical no doubt,
and your book says you
feel sorry for me and those
like me as you should.

We create as humans.
We consume as addicts.
I am tortured you see
living in both of these
self-justified conditions.

The words made by me
and others, all truths
from my glorified perceptions,
hold still, immobile
in my bomb shelter of a mind.

My made memories linger.
Their stories silent.
But they are still furrowed,
soundly. There is no light
in this Hell of a shelter.

I thought more than once
I had ahold of things,
but then realized I hold nothing.
You should feel sorry for me.

Post-Acute *(Day Nine)*

White-Knuckle it.

You have choices.

Bare down on this rotted stick.
Tilt back your head
and make sure your tongue
is still salty and oyster pink.
Stop flipping your eyes.
Just listen for the sound waves
or wait for smells of burnt cloth,
plastic, and feel your skin tickle, again.

I have white-knuckled it
for three days now.
My veins have closed off
to the voices
that say to surrender
is the honorable way out.
There are no purple hearts
here. Just poppy-eyed friends.

I have choices. Maybe tonight.

Day 10

The Chase

I am a trickster –

    Don't you see my powers?

I suppose not if you are too busy
chasing butterflies. I can manipulate
your life into my calculated desire.
Watch my hands pull out your heart

Don't forget to chase butterflies.

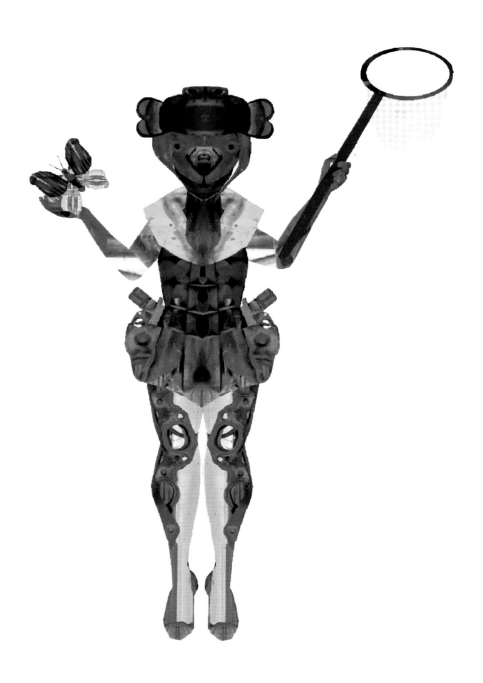

Dreams Never Mind (Day Eleven)

Dead hearts can caudle toxins.
Mine does, religiously.
Do not break bread for me.

Every night my dreams return
believing I never left. Episode
after episode -each believing
it is living. To them, my dreams,
something dead can always
be alive.

Our minds may be wondrous,
 but they are not mysterious-
controlled by instinct wrought
with insatiable desire.

I am my nightmare -
for I am the creator
of this mind. It grows,
thinks, and dies
on my command,
and even when
I kill cell by cell
the dead still stays
alive.

DAY 12

Play Your Part

There are miracles here amongst us.
They do not all see it, or even myself,
truly for that matter. Sometimes I feel it.

We are the protagonists of self-inflicting death.
Some of us prefer hypnotic, numbing methods
with needles to slide in moving targets.
Some of us drink our internal organs until
they are dry and useless.
Others of us prefer to defy the speed
of life by taking our minds higher than a god.
And then there are the others that
dig their flesh, swallow pills, and take packing
knives to their throats. It is death all the
same.

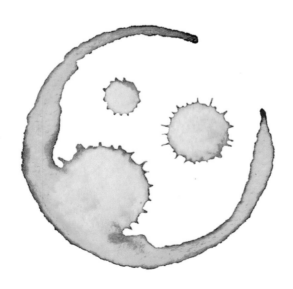

Perfect Feminine Form (Day Thirteen)

Create your body. Paint your pain,
paint what is inside of you. Use
colors. Use shapes.
Tell me what it means, she said.

First, I made a mouth.
I boxed over my uneven lips,
lined it in black and filled it
with yellow. I added squirms
of red trying to push it out.

The second part of myself I drew
were my eyes but they were not
as they should be. One eye was
charcoaled and lit with red. The
other eye was illuminated with purple
and blue refracting the iris.

Next, my most hated feature,
my nose. True to form,
zigzag and stuck sideways,
disturbed cartilage.

I made my hands plain, as I see them.
Lifeless, one finger chewed-up
and dead, the left-ring finger
just dangling there on paper.

My brain! Three parts, divided.

The far left: red
The middle: black
The far right: purple

I drew my wrists and inner thighs
like carved ham, pink and runny
with dark juicy red highlights. The
lines were serrated, sloppy marks.

Across my inner thighs I drew a triangle
for my vagina. A perfect model, the
perfect feminine form. But if you
looked more closely - there were
no openings.

Blood Orange Poppies (Day Fourteen)

His first sunset
was blood and ash
flashed through
a twisted tube.

Apollo now his God,
the sun inside of him
forever with just a needle
and a vein. How simple.

But elixirs lie, and
sunsets die everyday.
His pupils vanished
and so did all the beauty.

Until today, when his mother
looked into his eyes
and said, "Your pupils are beautiful"
A sunset, alive.

Asylum Irony (Day Fifteen)

In this room I cannot leave,
behind these walls that do not move,
stuck with doors that do not close,

watched by people day and night,
medicated, educated, facilitated,
regulated, delegated – there is freedom.

Day 16

Diseased

I do not know me anymore.
I am blank. Erased. Forgotten.
Blacked out.
Sober.
I wonder what lies are truths,
what truths are lies - and
which ones matter and which
ones will just disappear.
Or does my story
begin
 again
like it never started.
Did it start if it
was never real.
Before I was doing dirt -
I was already a disease.

Life Inside of Ashes (Day Seventeen)

I woke up this morning
a creature of Hell
lost from home.
There were no dreams
or memories to lead
me to how I got here –
in this strange place –
my body feeling
ackish, sluggish, a product
of pain and delusion.
I never was fire. I was always only ash.
How does ash become something else?

Grace (Day Eighteen)

My daughter said her sister
taught her everything.
Guilt does not even strike
a note to the emotion I bear.
There are no words; there are no definitions.

Did I stop loving them?
The very beings I pumped
blood into a cord that
grew their bodies gracefully
inside of me, a part of me.

How could I?

Day 19

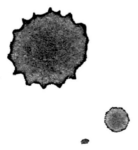

Demoralization

I am not different.

I am not a snowflake.

I am not uniquely unique.

I am an addict in the room.

I am an alcoholic in the room.

I have done things I cannot remember.

Just blackness.

I am from the blitz of failed living.

We all are. In these rooms.

Athena in the Shadows (Day Twenty)

She said there is a warrior
within you. You are strong.
You need to advocate for
yourself as strongly as you
do for all the others. You
suffer too. You are lucky
to be alive. Your higher power
was watching over you.
Do not hide anymore.

When you blink your eyes
I know you're holding back.
Stop. You need to grieve.
You are haunted. It is your
choice to live this way, or not.
You know what to do. You are
Athena. Trust your intuition.
She is inside of you. Always.

And I sit meek. I cannot accept
her words. Why? She says
because I am afraid, and I
asked of what. She said simply
of trusting someone, anyone.

And she is right.
I willingly, but unknowingly
trust no one.

Day 21

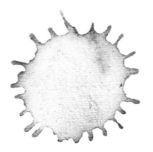

The Places We Go

He is just as much your addiction.
You have chosen him. I will never
see you again. Everyone warned
me – don't get too close. *Boundaries*
they said. *Pick the winners* they said.
I still picked you. I believed.

It is too quiet here without you.
Know that I still hear you.
Jails, institutions, and death.

Cunning (Day Twenty-Two)

I want to feel you.
A thousand of you would not suffice.
Your burn,
your taste,
your exuberance,
especially down my throat.
But I do not want you inside of me,
controlling me,
owning me,
changing me,
I do not want to feel you.
A thousand of you would not suffice.

A Snake in the Grass (Day Twenty-Three)

my brain tells me to send
     you up, up, up and away
     in my nose you go!

you slither up there
     slippery and fast
     shedding my thin skin open.

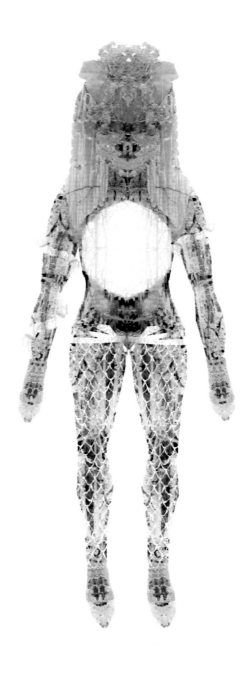

Facades (Day Twenty-Four)

I could perform my cover well.
Rehearsal was survival and
I was the fittest.
Your performances,
however,
never measured. I sat and
judged. Your authenticity
popped like bubble gum.

Day 25

The Nights Edge

Dreams have watermarks,
traceable, detectable —
each inexplicably marked.
Every dream
has lines and edges.

I have one dream for most nights,
and two dreams for lonely nights.

I wait for the edgeless nights,
where the lines cannot find me.

A Mother Knows (Day Twenty-Six)

I took my mother to the concrete room
so she could learn about my disease.
She was going to hear I was an alcoholic
and an addict for the first time from
my first-born lips.

She said,

"These tears are happy tears.
I finally have hope that you
will live past me. A child should
always out live their parents. My
deepest fear is the you would
be dead before me – I have
felt that way for a long time."

I never knew she could see
my death. A mother knows.

Day 27

Gray Matter

There is gray matter
inside my head –
fissured with time
by people who live still
through me, around me
and I just watch, dull
with eyes stuffed and
made of glass. They
were placed and glazed
for this purpose. To never
even blink when a fly
tramples across them.

My creature eyes are
unoiled axels that jerk
bringing me back to
terrifying, joyous life.
The gray matter is alive.

Bottles & Bones (Day Twenty-Eight)

Bottles.
Artifacts, my legacy.
I stowed them carelessly.
Brown, green, clear with a blue goose.
Every bottle had become a bone,
dry, my relics I coveted while full
and despised empty. They meant
nothing empty. A body without
flesh means nothing – it is just
empty bones.

I tasted too many bones
that I could even find empty.

Day 29

Culprit

Dopamine levels. Serotonin levels.
Limbic System. Frontal Lobe.
Drugs had taken mine hostage!
Again, I robbed myself.
No one can arrest my disease.

Window Watching (Day Thirty)

When a leaf begins to crisp does it feel?
I saw you changing from green to brown.
Your veins, drying, tightening. You can
no longer hold water – your only life source.
We all watched you die. We called you
beautiful before you changed. Crest-fallen,
you hit the ground. Dramatic. The sun
reading your veins like Braille one last time
until we rake you up and throw you away.

Lindsay Gargotto earned an MFA at Spalding University in Louisville, KY after serving in the United States Air Force. She is the Founder and Executive Director of Athena's Sisters - an organization that provides healing and artistic advocacy for military women. She is also the editor of *WarrioHer*, the only national publication pen to print by military women, which her work appears in. She is the mother of two beautiful and brilliant daughters - Kyleigh and Kady.

Bree is a Pleasureville, KY artist and poet who recieved an Artist Enrichment Grant in visual arts from the Kentucky Foundation for Women in 2016. Each of her collages is made from a single photograph on Paint; she often uses Fotor, Photos or Adobe Photoshop Express to enhance a finished image.

Collages in order of appearance:

Bull Moon Risin 11.4.16 Collage made from a single photograph taken in Pleasureville, KY made on Paint, enhanced with Photos. (front cover)

Day One 6.19.17 Collage made from a single photograph of a sunset in Christianburg, KY made on Paint, enhanced with Adobe Photoshop Express to illustrate a book of poems written during the first 30 days of a female veteran's recovery.

Awakening 1.15.17 Collage made from a photograph of a crush aerosol can in Pleasureville, KY made on Paint, enhanced with Fotor and Photos.

Owl Wouldja Please 9.19.16 Collage made from a single photograph of an Owl Butterfly, from the Naturalist's Notebook taken by John Pizniur.

Catching Butterflies 6.21.17 Collage made from a single photograph taken in a farm shed in Waddy, KY made on Paint, enhanced with Adobe Photoshop Express.

Water is Solace 5.18.17 Collage made from single photograph of motorcycle boots taken in Waddy, KY made on Paint.

Brain is a Moving Target 6.21.17 Collage made from a single photograph of a sunset in Bagdag, KY made on Paint.

What Can i Say, i'm Hooked 6.4.17 Collage made from a single photograph of a coat rack from a brothel torn down in Waddy, KY, made on Paint, enhanced with Adobe Photoshop Express.

Naagi Mani 11.8.16 Collage made from a single photograph of Muskatatuck forest made on Paint, enhanced with Fotor. Naagi are female cobras who can take human form if they have lived for 100 yrs, and may possess a gem much more precious than a diamond.

Night Terror 5.21.17 Collage made from a single photograph of a dust bunny taken in Waddy, KY made on Paint, enhanced with Adobe Photoshop Express.

Queen of Flies 6.23.17 Collage made from a single photograph of red and blue peeling paint taken in Shelbyville, KY made on Paint, enhanced with Adobe Photoshop Express. (Back Cover)

73590081R00036

Made in the USA
Columbia, SC
13 July 2017